ST. ALBANS CATHEDRAL

ABOVE: *The cathedral from the south west.* FACING PAGE: *One of two survivors of the many brasses which were in St. Albans Abbey. It shows the knight, Sir Antony Grey, a relation of Edward IV. This brass is in front of the altar rail on the south side. The other surviving brass, that of Thomas de la Mare is shown on page 18.*

TOP: *The Benedictine Abbey of St. Albans founded in 793. This drawing* *shows the Abbey as it was prior to the Dissolution in 1539.* ABOVE: *St. Albans Cathedral from Verulamium.*

ST. ALBANS CATHEDRAL

D. R. FEAVER

A CHURCH from about 300 A.D., an abbey from 793 to 1539, a cathedral from 1877, but still known locally as The Abbey, the Cathedral and Abbey Church of St. Alban stands on a hill overlooking the site of the once famous Roman city of Verulamium. It marks the place where the first man in this island to die for the Christian Faith was martyred. He was a Roman soldier, called Alban, stationed in Verulamium. He died, most probably, some time between 303* and 305 in the last years of the reign of the Emperor Diocletian, who promulgated two edicts against the Christians in 303.

The story of Alban's martyrdom runs as follows. During a persecution of the Christians he, a pagan, gave shelter to a fugitive Christian priest, and was by him baptized. When the soldiers came to Alban's house, he changed clothes with his guest, and was taken by the soldiers to the magistrate who was in the act of sacrificing to idols. Alban was questioned about his new-found beliefs. "I am called Alban," he replied, "and I worship and adore the true and living God who created all things." He was condemned to death as a dog unfit to live; and was taken out of the town, across the river, and up onto the hill where his church now stands, and there he was beheaded.

These seem to be the bare facts. By the time the Abbey chronicler, Matthew Paris, wrote them up in the middle of the thirteenth century, they had attracted to themselves many embellishments. The shadowy priest,

*

ABOVE, right: *A representation of St. Matthew in the west porch. The features are Lord Grimthorpe's, the nineteenth-century restorer of the Abbey.*

* *Later research, still continuing, indicates that the martyrdom was in 209 A.D., earlier than the Diocletian reign.*

to whom Alban gave shelter, is given a name, Amphibalus. The heavens are filled with wondrous signs, and the headsman who killed Alban is smitten down, and then restored to life by touching the saint's body. Bede's account in his *Ecclesiastical History,* upon which Matthew Paris relies, was written about 730. It includes one or two modest miracles, and is particularly important in that it indicates that in Bede's own day the site of Alban's martyrdom was well known, and that there was a church on the spot, which was famous for works of healing.

Venantius Fortunatus, Bishop of Poitiers (*circa* 600) wrote many well known hymns. Among them are "The royal banners forward go", and "Sing, my tongue, the glorious battle". He also wrote a long poem in praise of Virginity, in which he lists famous martyrs, St. Cyprian, St. Vincent and

St. Victor, and, with them, St. Alban in the line;

"*Egregium Albanum fecunda Britannia profert*"

which may be translated,
"First of the noble host in
Britain's land (Mother of Saints)
see glorious Alban stand."

St. Germanus, Bishop of Auxerre, in the early fifth century dedicated one of his churches in honour of St. Alban. One account of the *Life of St. Germanus* mentions a pilgrimage which he made to Britain when he visited St. Alban's grave and deposited relics in it. There seems to be no reason to doubt Gildas when he wrote that after the persecutions British Christians were careful to build churches in honour of their martyred brethren. Gildas wrote about 550; and it may be that his account of Alban's martyrdom, conjoined with

his statement about the pious building of churches, can be taken as evidence that there was a church of St. Alban on the site of his martyrdom within a very few years of his death.

The official founder of the Abbey of St. Alban is usually reckoned to be Offa of Mercia in the eighth century. Matthew Paris makes much of Offa. He quotes charters purported to have been granted by him, conferring great privileges and exemptions from royal and episcopal authority. They are patently fictitious. But behind the fancies there is a trace of truth. Offa translated the bones of St. Alban into a more splendid sepulchre; he built a new church, and put regular monks in charge of it, and endowed the convent with lands which lie immediately round St. Albans in a compact estate. This last suggests that the Abbey received the nucleus of its endowments before the Norman Conquest. After the Conquest it was not so easy for a patron to find lands close to the monastery he wished to endow.

The bulk of the church, as the visitor sees it today, was built by the first Norman abbot, Paul of Caen. He was a great friend of Archbishop Lanfranc, and full of the zeal of reorganisation. He reformed the monks by making them wear a seemly monastic habit, and sing tunefully the new chants imported from the Continent. He saw that they kept silence, when silence was required, in the cloister and in the dormitory. Within eleven years of becoming abbot in 1077 he had rebuilt the whole church, except the bakehouse

Continued on page 6

*

LEFT: *The Nave, looking east, showing the high altar and reredos beyond the nave screen. Three architectural styles can be seen: in the foreground, Early English; behind, on the north side, the original eleventh-century Norman, and on the south side, five bays of Decorated.*

ABOVE, right: *The first painting from which wax and dirt were removed in 1955. The freshness and vigour of the original drawings are brought out. All the paintings in the nave and two in the transepts have been similarly treated.*

RIGHT: *Thirteenth and fourteenth-century paintings. On the west side of the piers are pictures of the Crucifixion: on the south sides St. Christopher can just be recognised on the first pier and St. Thomas of Canterbury on the second.*

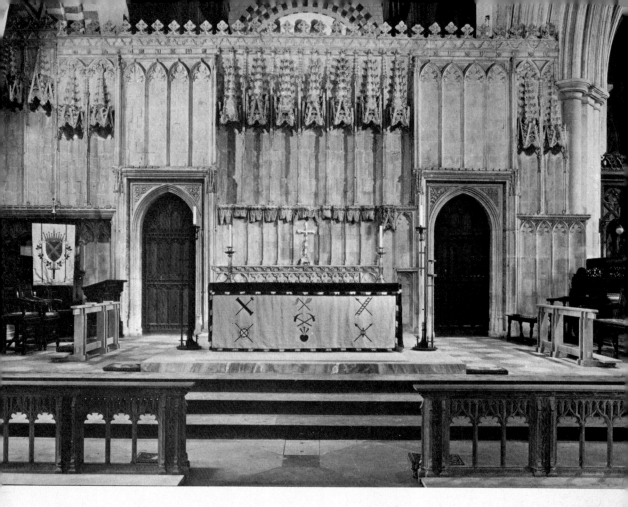

and buttery which he found in good order. He had the utmost contempt for the ways and works of his Saxon predecessors. *"Rudes et idiotas"*, he called them. His massive, dull edifice typified the heavy, arrogant hand of the Normans upon all things English.

Paul's church must have given just that impression. If the visitor today stands inside the west door and looks east, he sees the great round arches under the tower. Beyond them the original Norman church ended in an apse where the present high altar is. The whole of the structure looked like the nine bays which now remain west of the tower on the north side. The building virtually consisted of four parallel walls running west to east, with the inner pair pierced by round-headed openings.

There is no building stone in St. Albans except flint, which is difficult to use. So Paul, and his Saxon predecessors, collected bricks from the ruins of pagan Verulamium and built them into the Christian church. Roman sites in the neighbourhood have provided a quarry for building repairs ever since. The tower, which is most people's first glimpse of the Abbey from far away, is made of bricks almost twice as old as itself.

Inside the church the bricks were covered with plaster which was painted. On some of the piers in the nave the paintings have reappeared since the middle of the nineteenth century from under the puritanic whitewash. They are thirteenth and fourteenth-century, and were done by a group of painters who gave St. Albans a high reputation. The cleaning of the murals begun in 1955 shows the sensitiveness of the original drawings. The murals on the west sides of the pillars portray the Cruci-fixion in the upper panels, and the Blessed Virgin Mary in the lower. The south faces show (from west to east) St. Christopher, the patron of pilgrims; St. Thomas of Canterbury, the medieval ecclesiastical hero whom Henry VIII abhorred (St. Thomas's face has been patriotically rubbed out); St. Osyth, and, maybe, St. Edward the Confessor.

A major rebuilding and extension was begun just before 1200 by Abbot John de Cella. It went on in fits and

Continued on page 8

★

ABOVE: *The nave screen, or pulpitum, which was built by Thomas de la Mare (1350). The figures of the saints were removed during the Reformation. The processional doors are original. The altar cross is a piece of Spanish crystal work of the time of Philip II.*

RIGHT: *The organ was rebuilt in 1962 and is a fine example of modern, tonal design. Internationally famous organists regularly give recitals on it. The north and south cases are by John Oldred Scott and date from 1908. The central case was completed in 1962 to a design by Cecil Brown, F.R.I.B.A.*

starts until the year before Magna Carta. The Abbey was by then rich enough to import stone. The bishops, magnates, and sheriffs summoned to the Council of St. Albans in August 1213 would have seen the western bays of the nave much as the visitor today finds them. They are a monument to the vagaries of medieval mathematics, and to those whom the Lord's parable describes as building a tower without sitting down first to count the cost. Before the introduction of Arabic numerals, arithmetic was often inexact. A glance at the unfinished western bays and the inside of the west wall shows the consequence of such inexactitude.

The five bays on the south side and the four on the north are simple strong structures, with deep cut mouldings, dog-tooth ornament, and bisected triforium arcading. But the springers show that a vault was intended, and the empty bases for marble shafts on the inside of the west wall suggest that the builders' money, or courage, or both, failed. Abbot William of Trumpington had patched up the west end by 1235; but St. Albans had to wait for the nineteenth century and Lord Grimthorpe to give it a complete west end; and his façade has called more for censure than for commendation.

In 1323 five bays on the south side, just west of the nave screen, collapsed. They were rebuilt somewhat leisurely because one of the abbots, Richard of Wallingford, was more interested in perfecting his astronomical clock than in church building. By the middle of the century, the five bays were reconstructed, and they are the finest range in the church; fairly elaborate, with lavish ball-flower decoration, intricate shallow mouldings, and on the head mouldings very fine portraits in stone of the abbot, Hugh of Eversden, Queen Isabella (her cherubic cheeks

Continued on page 10

★

LEFT: *The north transept. Lord Grimthorpe designed and erected the window. The arches of the central tower are as their builder, Paul of Caen, left them.*

RIGHT: *The nave, looking west. This picture, taken from the organ loft, shows Lord Grimthorpe's west window which was filled with stained glass (by Comper) in memory of those from the diocese who gave their lives in World War I. The wooden ceiling is nineteenth-century.*

belie her reputation), Edward II, and the Master of the Works.

The nave screen was put up a few years later. This also has a delightful disregard for mathematics. Nothing is in the middle of anything else, and the axis of the screen is not at right angles to the line of the nave. Fortunately St. Albans Abbey has never fallen for the fatal fascination of vistas which has opened up, and so ruined, so many abbeys and cathedrals to make of two interior churches one vast elongated tunnel.

The choir, which lies east of the nave screen, or pulpitum, and within the architectural nave itself, is the place where the praises of God are, and were, sung daily. The canons' stalls date from the beginning of the present century. They are named after worthies connected with the Abbey. They take the place of the monks' stalls, which continued through the tower crossing, blocking the transepts, and dominated on the east by the Saint's shrine with the high altar in front of it. At least, that is how it was until 1484 when the present reredos was erected. There is one other screen like it, at Winchester. It has been much restored, notably by the first Lord Aldenham, about 1900, when he refilled the niches with a multitude of mediocre figures representing famous people connected in fact, or in imagination, with the Abbey. The high screen dominates the central part of the Abbey, and holds the attention of the worshipper in the presbytery.

The transepts are full of Lord Grimthorpe's misdeeds. The north transept is lighted by his "banker's window". The circular shapes of the glass correspond to the sizes of coins of the realm. The south transept is cowed by the five gargantuan lancets which Grimthorpe put there instead of a temporary wooden framed window, which replaced the perpendicular window blown down in a storm in 1703. Below the lancets is a Norman door reversed and augmented by Grimthorpe, leading into a passage which ran from the transept to the vanished chapter house, and called the slype.

No visitor to the Abbey must fail to penetrate the Saint's chapel which is behind the high altar. From the Reformation until the end of the nineteenth century its eastern arches were blocked by rubble, and the Grammar School inhabited the Lady Chapel beyond. The School was removed and settled in the great gateway which is part of its home today: the footpath which ran behind the Saint's chapel was closed, and the arches were opened. In doing this work about two thousand pieces of the pedestal, upon which rested the reliquary containing the relics of St. Alban, were found and pieced together to form about a third of the structure of the original. The result is enough to show what the former glory must have been like when, before the high screen was built, the shrine standing on the highest ground in the Abbey was to be seen from the choir, lucent with gems and silver gilt, and towering above the high altar. There are still traces of colour on the marble of the pedestal. The west face shows the martyrdom; the south the royal founder, Offa, holding the church in his hand; the east St. Alban's flagellation. The back of the high screen is as fine in its simplicity as the front is in its richness.

Humphrey of Gloucester's tomb, on the south side of the shrine, makes a silent commentary on the Reformation: the royal arms are left intact; elsewhere the figures of the Saints have gone.

On the north side is the Watching Chamber made of wood (about 1400). In it sat a monk to watch over the shrine and the continual flow of pilgrims who came (and still come, especially in June, St. Albanstide) to make their offering and to say their prayers. It is a rare and fine piece of woodwork, well preserved because for many years after the Reformation the chapel was the vestry and inaccessible to the meddling fingers of

Continued on page 18

⋆

ABOVE, left: *The Triforium, built in the time of King John. The arcading is most graceful. Note the dog-tooth ornamentation, the deeply-cut mouldings of the arches and, in the clerestory, the detached shafts. A roof vault was intended; the bases of the springers can be seen.*

LEFT: *The pillars in the Triforium of the south transept are monoliths and the only bits of the Saxon church to be used by the Norman rebuilders.*

RIGHT: *The south ambulatory. This picture shows the variety of vaulting in the south choir aisle and nave aisle. The Norman arch, and vaulting in the middle distance, are ancient.*

LEFT: *This view of the high altar from the choir shows the Bishop's Throne (right), the Norman arches of the tower crossing, a glimpse of the Saxon pilasters in the north transept, the presbytery with thirteenth-century wooden vaulted roof, and reredos dating from the fifteenth century with figures restored at a later date.*

ABOVE: *The reredos was completed in 1484 by Abbot William of Wallingford and cost eleven hundred marks. The panel above the altar represents the Resurrection. It was made by Sir Alfred Gilbert, R.A.*

ABOVE: *Panels of the choir ceiling which has remained almost untouched since the fifteenth century, although for a time it was plastered over.*

RIGHT: *The north ambulatory. St. Michael's Chapel was restored in 1927 in memory of those who fell in World War I. The outside of the Ramryge*

Chapel is seen on the right; it is on the north side of the sanctuary, and was the last work to be carried out in the Abbey before the Dissolution.

ABOVE: *The Ramryge Chantry. Abbot Ramryge died in 1521. It is probable that there were never any statues in the niches. The abbot's rebus is repeated round the walls—a ram with a collar and the letters R Y G E.*

LEFT: *The Shrine of St. Alban. The pieces outlining the pedestal of the shrine were found in 1872 in a wall which blocked the arches at the east end of the Chapel. The pedestal is of Purbeck marble and is covered with* carvings of scenes from Alban's martyrdom. *The recesses contain some of the original colouring. Beyond the pedestal is the early fifteenth-century watching chamber from which the shrine was guarded.*

mischief makers. The back of the chamber is carved with vignettes of scenes from rural life. The Saint's chapel was the reason for the Abbey's existence and the centre of its fame and glory.

In December 1539 the last abbot, Richard Borman, and thirty-eight monks surrendered the house into the hands of Henry VIII. Sir Richard Lee got hold of the buildings, and knocked them all down except the gateway and the church. The foundations of the tower were undermined, and the shell of the church was sold to the towns-people for £400 to be their parish church. The ancient parish church of St. Andrew, which was adjacent to the north wall of the nave, disappeared.

For the next three hundred years the history of the Abbey is the chronicle of a handful of parishioners trying to keep in repair a building far too big for them. By the end they were using only the presbytery and part of the north transept until the great restoration and rebuilding began. The Abbey is still a parish church. In 1877 it became also the cathedral of the new diocese of St. Albans which now comprises the counties of Hertford and Bedford. In 1900 the rector became titular dean. In 1938 the cathedral received statutes, and provision was made for the establishment of residentiary canons. So in its long history the church has been a rude chapel wherein to preserve the proto-martyr's relics, an abbey of the first rank, a deserted ruin, a parish church, and, now too, a cathedral.

The history of the Abbey is punctuated by a very few eminent names. Nicholas Breakspeare was born within the liberty of St. Albans, and, as a youth, he was refused admission

Continued on page 21

★

LEFT: *One of the most magnificent brasses in existence. This brass of Thomas de la Mare shows him as a young man in all his priestly and abbatical dignity. It was made by a Flemish artist about 1360.*

RIGHT: *Humphrey of Gloucester's tomb. Humphrey Duke of Gloucester, brother of Henry V, was a friend of the abbot of St. Albans. He is buried close by the martyr's shrine and his tomb is built in such a way as not to obscure the pilgrims' view of the shrine as they went through the ambulatory.*

as a novice. In 1154 he was elected Pope as Adrian IV, the only Englishman ever to be Bishop of Rome. His election gave the Abbey its great chance; and Adrian's Bull *Incomprehensibilis* gave St. Albans a pre-eminence which it kept to the end of its monastic days. The abbot ranked above all English abbots. The monastery was exempt from all visitations save that of a *legatus a latere*: the authority of the Bishop of Lincoln over the convent and the parishes in the Liberty was abolished.

Matthew Paris the chronicler has been mentioned. He was one of the most colourful personalities connected with the Abbey. He became a monk in 1217, and died, probably, in 1259. Eighteen of his manuscripts survive, but not in St. Albans. The most famous are *Chronica Majorca, Flores Historiarum, Gesta Abbatum* and *Historia Anglorum.* St. Albans is twenty miles from London along Watling Street, about as far as a horse can carry a man comfortably in a day. The monks of the Abbey were in a good position to collect news and gossip from their guests. Kings, queens, papal legates, bishops and royal agents continually called or stayed in the guest chambers. Matthew made the most of what he heard, and spiced it thoroughly with prejudices, and leavened it with a persistent sense of his own importance. He had a perpetual grudge against all kinds of authority, especially the Pope's, and could never resist telling a disreputable tale about papal enormities. He was a personal friend of Henry III. He could draw, not without a trick of caricature; he shows Henry with a drooping eyelid. Heraldry, cartography and hagiology were his hobbies. His foibles and scandals make as good reading today as they ever did.

Continued on page 22

★

RIGHT: *This medieval painting of William Fitzherbert, Archbishop of York in the reign of Stephen, is on the arcading east of the shrine, where the arches were bricked up for 300 years after the Dissolution. Some of the medieval colouring has survived.*

LEFT: *The Retro-choir. Before the Lady Chapel was built these arches terminated the east end of the Abbey. From Edward VI until 70 years ago a footpath went through the retro-choir and separated the School in the Lady Chapel from the rest of the Abbey.*

The very greatest of the abbots was Thomas de la Mare. He died in 1396, aged 87, having been abbot for forty seven years. He was, unlike his predecessors, of an aristocratic family. He was an accomplished preacher, and most scrupulous in requiring a devout and unhurried performance of the liturgy and of the psalms. He was a friend of the Black Prince, a Privy Councillor, and a friend of the French King John who

*

was for a time a prisoner in St. Albans. He did all the things expected of a great abbot. He built the gatehouse and lavished treasures and ornaments upon the church, and was insistent upon his position as abbot of the premier abbey of England. Behind all his official magnificence was severe self-discipline. He ate but once a day: he always wore a hair shirt: whenever he had half an hour to spare he would recite the Office for the Dead. He heard three Masses a day and never failed to rise at midnight to say the Night Office. He would tend the sick with his own hands, and in his last long lingering illness, he preferred the ministrations of his monks to those of the medical profession. His abbacy marked the great days of the monastery, and his life is one of the very best examples of a monk's vocation faithfully followed.

The only other abbot whose name

is known outside St. Albans is John Bostock of Wheathampstead. He was twice abbot. He was born in 1393. At Gloucester Hall, Oxford, he showed considerable brilliance and promise. At twenty-seven he was elected abbot, but his reign was curiously disappointing. He resigned in 1441 on the ground that he could not control his blushes when he heard obscene
Continued on page 24

*

remarks in public. He soon returned to be abbot again in time to repair the damage made to Abbey property by the victors of the second Battle of St. Albans, after which the convent dispersed for a time. He was a friend of Humphrey, Duke of Gloucester, and was mildly interested in the New Learning.

The latter part of the nineteenth century was dominated in St. Albans by a formidable man who became the first Baron Grimthorpe. He was born Edmund Beckett Denison, son of a railway king. He became Sir Edmund Becket, Bart. He was chancellor and vicar general of York, an amateur clock maker (he made Big Ben), an amateur architect and the enemy of all professionals, medical and architectural; a habitual restorer of churches, a millionaire, and a man of, what are politely called in ecclesiastical circles, pronounced views. This meant that he hated deans and chapters, Puseyites, and statues (which he always called idols). This did not stop him allowing his own features to represent St. Matthew in a carving in the west porch. He arrived one day in St. Albans when a committee was sitting to discover ways and means of

repairing the Abbey. He came to the rescue and restored the building at his own expense, and, naturally, to his own specifications. Many hard things have been said about him, as he said many hard things about others. He will continue to be criticised as long as his west front, his transept windows, his pepperpots, and his alpine treatment of the outside of the Lady Chapel survive; and that will be for a very long time. None of his work is banal. It may be showy and vulgar. He saved the church from falling into ruins, and made it weatherproof and structurally sound. St. Albans owes him much.

*   *   *

The history of the Abbey from Paul of Caen to the Reformation follows the pattern of most great monastic houses. There were conflicts with the townspeople; arguments about precedence and exemptions; troubles with popes, kings, friars and tax collectors. In its great days in the thirteenth century it numbered a hundred monks. In the late Middle Ages it shared the universal difficulty of attracting young

men of adventure who preferred the foreign wars to the specialised spiritual struggle of the religious. The Abbey made a continual fight against a faulty economy which stayed rigid in the face of changing conditions.

*   *   *

ABOVE: *The Gatehouse is late fourteenth century and is the sole survivor of the monastic buildings. In Mary Tudor's time it was used as a gaol and continued as such until occupied by the School in 1871. The upper rooms have been restored and furnished by St. Albans school as a war memorial.*

BACK COVER: *The Norman Tower of St. Albans.*

Acknowledgments

All the colour pictures in this book, with the exception of the front cover which is by A. F. Kersting, A.I.I.P., F.R.P.S., are by S. W. Newbery, Hon.F.I.I.P., F.R.P.S. All the black and white pictures, with the exception of a few by S. W. Newbery, are by Margaret F. Harker, F.I.I.P., Hon.F.R.P.S., F.R.S.A.

SBN 85372 057 6